# CHANGING PLANET

What is the environmental impact of
human migration and settlement?

By Sally Morgan

# Crabtree Publishing Company
## www.crabtreebooks.com

**Author**: Sally Morgan
**Project director**: Ruth Owen
**Designer**: Elaine Wilkinson
**Editors**: Mark Sachner, Lynn Peppas
**Proofreader:** Molly Aloian
**Editorial director:** Kathy Middleton
**Prepress technician:** Katherine Berti
**Production coordinator:** Margaret Amy Salter
**Consultant**: Ceri Oeppen BSc, MSc, of the Sussex
Centre for Migration Research

**Front cover (top)**: In newly industrialized countries, such as India and China, cities are growing fast. Here, construction is completed on the Shanghai World Financial Center in Shanghai, China.
**Front cover (bottom left):** A truck is loaded with trees cut down in a rain forest.
**Front cover (bottom center):** In some major cities cars choke the roads pumping carbon emissions and pollution into the atmosphere 24 hours a day.
**Front cover (bottom right):** Dust Bowl migrant Florence Owens Thompson.
**Back cover:** New road construction underway in Chongqing, China. The area's economy is growing fast—especially its automobile industry.
**Title page:** Here, the capital city of Japan, Tokyo, spreads for many miles into the distance. Tokyo has the largest population of any city in the world—over 35 million people live in the city center and suburbs.

**Photo credits:**
Alamy: page 24 (bottom, top left); Galen Rowell: page 32 (bottom); Paul Doyle: page 34
Adrian Arbib: page 31 (bottom)
Corbis: Patrick Robert: pages 11 (top), 12 (bottom); Patrick Robert: pages 15, 17 (top); Sandy Stockwell: pages 18 (bottom), 19 (bottom); Michael Reynolds: page 29 (top)
Dockside Green: pages 38–39
Ecoscene: pages 8 (bottom), 9, 12 (top), 24–25 (center), 29 (bottom), 31 (top), 41, 43
Getty Images: Paula Bronstein: pages 10–11 (center); Paula Bronstein: page 16 (bottom); pages 20–21 (center)
Last Refuge: page 6
Library of Congress: front cover (bottom right), pages 3 (center left), 13, 19 (top)
Ruby Tuesday Books Ltd: pages 10 (top), 16 (top)
Science Photo Library: page 4 (bottom)
Shutterstock: front cover (top, bottom left, bottom center), back cover, pages 1, 3 (left), 3 (center right), 3 (right), 4 (left), 5, 7, 8 (left all), 14, 18 (left), 20 (bottom), 21 (bottom right), 22–23, 24 (bottom, top right), 24 (bottom left), 24 (bottom right), 25 (center), 26–27, 28, 30, 33 (top), 35, 36–37, 42
Wikipedia (public domain): pages 21 (bottom left), 32 (top), 33 (bottom), 40

Developed & Created for Crabtree Publishing Company by Ruby Tuesday Books Ltd

### Library and Archives Canada Cataloguing in Publication

Morgan, Sally
    Changing planet : what is the environmental impact of human migration and settlement? / Sally Morgan.

(Investigating human migration & settlement)
Includes index.
ISBN 978-0-7787-5179-3 (bound).--ISBN 978-0-7787-5194-6 (pbk.)

    1. Emigration and immigration--Environmental aspects--Juvenile literature. 2. Human settlements--Environmental aspects--Juvenile literature. 3. Cities and towns--Growth--Juvenile literature. 4. Land use--Environmental aspects--Juvenile literature. I. Title. II. Series: Investigating human migration & settlement

HB1952.M67 2010          j333.7          C2009-905268-7

### Library of Congress Cataloging-in-Publication Data

Morgan, Sally.
 Changing planet : what is the environmental impact of human migration and settlement? / by Sally Morgan.
    p. cm. -- (Investigating human migration & settlement)
 Includes index.
 ISBN 978-0-7787-5194-6 (pbk. : alk. paper) -- ISBN 978-0-7787-5179-3 (reinforced library binding : alk. paper)
 1. Migration, Internal--Juvenile literature. 2. Emigration and immigration--Juvenile literature. 3. Human settlements--Juvenile literature. 4. Cities and towns--Growth--Juvenile literature. 5. Land use--Environmental aspects--Juvenile literature. I. Title. II. Series.

HB1952.M67 2010
333.77--dc22
                                        2009034888

## Crabtree Publishing Company
www.crabtreebooks.com          1-800-387-7650

Printed in China/122009/CT20090915

**Published in Canada**
**Crabtree Publishing**
616 Welland Ave.
St. Catharines, ON
L2M 5V6

**Published in the United States**
**Crabtree Publishing**
PMB 59051
350 Fifth Avenue, 59th Floor
New York, New York 10118

**Published in the United Kingdom**
**Crabtree Publishing**
Maritime House
Basin Road North, Hove
BN41 1WR

**Published in Australia**
**Crabtree Publishing**
386 Mt. Alexander Rd.
Ascot Vale (Melbourne)
VIC 3032

# CONTENTS

▼ *The Sahara Desert in North Africa is the world's largest desert. It covers an area of nearly 3.5 million square miles (9 million sq km). Around 125,000 years ago, temporary changes in climate caused this area to cool and become lush with plant life and water. During this time, our ancestors in Africa made their first attempts to migrate—the Sahara became a gateway to the rest of the world.*

# CHAPTER ONE

# PEOPLE ON THE MOVE

Around the world, people are on the move. Each day, people leave their homes to travel to work or school. Some travel further for vacations or business. Others make permanent moves to live in other places. These movements can damage environments—both local environments and the global environment.

▲ *This artwork of an early modern human (Homo sapiens sapiens) shows a man teaching young boys how to make stone spearheads for catching fish. In the background is a simple shelter with a wood (or bone) framework and a covering made from animal skins. This shelter would have been easy to dismantle when it was time for the group to move on.*

## Our Ancestors on the Move

The first migrations of modern humans took place around 150,000 years ago when our ancestors began to move around the continent of Africa. Then, around 125,000 years ago, they started to move out of Africa. Over tens of thousands of years, humans spread across the world, moving first into Asia, then Europe and later into the Americas, and Australia. These people used flakes of rock to make tools such as spears for hunting and choppers to fell trees. Their simple hunter-gatherer lifestyle and low population numbers made only very small changes to their surroundings.

4

## The First Settlements

For thousands of years humans were hunter-gatherers. They lived together in small groups moving around—with no fixed settlements—hunting animals, and gathering plant foods. Then, about 13,000 to 10,000 years ago, people started to keep animals and grow plants for food. This was a major change as it meant people had to settle in one place. Historians are unsure what caused this change, but droughts could have led to a shortage of wild grasses and other plants, so people started to grow their own. The farmers cleared land to make way for crops, while trees were felled for fuel and to make shelters. The regular supply of food allowed the population to grow, and people lived longer. When there were too many people in a settlement, some would leave and set up new settlements. This migration to new areas continues today, for a variety of other reasons.

## Resources for Settlements

People need a supply of fresh water so many settlements were built beside rivers and lakes. As settlements grew over time, demands for other resources grew. More trees were felled for timber, and rocks and sand were dug from the ground for use in building homes and animal pens and for laying paths. People produced waste, too—sewage and garbage—which could be dumped in a nearby river to be carried away. All these activities had an impact on the surrounding environment.

# FOCUS ON:

## WHAT IS MIGRATION?

Human migration is the movement of groups of people from one place in the world to another for the same reason. Migration can be voluntary because people have chosen to move, but it can also be forced, due to war or environmental disasters. Migration can involve travel between continents or just within the same country. During the 1500s and 1600s, migrants left Europe to travel to the Americas, or "New World," in search of gold and silver, or more land and a better life. Today in China, millions of people are leaving their rural homes to live in cities where they hope to find better jobs, and are able to send money home to support their families.

◄ ▲ *Some migrations are daily, such as commuting—traveling between home and work. Others are seasonal, when people travel on vacation and then return home.*

## Creating Artificial Landscapes

In densely populated regions such as Northern Europe and parts of South East Asia, much of the landscape has been artificially created by people. The wild forests that once covered much of Europe 5,000 years ago are gone, and in their place are managed landscapes of farmland, grassland, and heathland. Many of the woodlands in Britain were planted by people hundreds of years ago to make sure there was a steady supply of timber. In Southeast Asia, whole hillsides have been terraced to grow rice, creating a unique landscape.

## Living in Harmony

▲ *A Waorani hunter returns from a hunting trip having killed a toucan using a blowpipe (top). When moving to a new area of the forest, the Waorani burn their hut and build a new one at the new settlement.*

Not all humans are impacting the environment. Some groups of people live lives that are in harmony with their local environment.

Many indigenous people live in the world's rain forests—the dense tropical forests that are found near the equator. The rain forests provide the people with all that they need to survive. Some tribes, such as the Waorani Indians of the Ecuadorian rain forest, are nomadic people who

6

do very little damage to the forest. They are hunter-gatherers who move around the forest collecting fruits and plants, and hunting for animal prey such as birds and monkeys.

Other tribes, such as the Kayapo people in the Amazonian rain forest of Brazil, make permanent settlements and they tend to have more impact on their surroundings. They settle in one place and clear larger areas of the forest by "slash and burn" to grow crops. They also cut down trees for fuel and shelters and they may keep animals such as chickens and pigs. After about four or five years, they move to another area.

## Modern Settlements and Their Environmental Impact

Our modern lives are far more technically advanced than those of our ancestors but the need for resources, and often the need to settle close to these resources, has continued. Unfortunately, today, our settlements —towns, cities, and industrial areas—are impacting not just the local environment, like those of our ancestors, but the global environment, too. Our increasing demand for food and wood has resulted in the destruction of rain forests, while the burning of fossil fuels, such as oil and coal, is causing pollution and global warming. The resources we rely on in our modern lives, such as fossil fuels, iron ore, and other minerals, are all in demand and their extraction has an impact on the environment.

However, there is a demand for change especially among younger people. The race is on to find renewable energy sources such as wind power and solar power.

## THE SOUTH DOWNS

The South Downs of Southern England were once covered by trees, but the landscape has long since been cleared of forests and in their place are open grassy hills. The grassland, or downland, has to be managed or it would revert to forest, so the land is grazed by sheep and cattle to keep the grass short and free of tree seedlings.

▼ The South Downs are a range of chalk hills approximately 106 miles (170 km) long and three miles (5 km) wide. The clearance of trees on the Downs began around 5,000 to 6,000 years ago. Initially, people enlarged existing forest clearings in order to graze livestock.

# CHAPTER TWO
# DISAPPEARING HABITATS

About 15 percent of Earth's land was once covered by tropical rain forest. Sadly, less than half the rain forests remain, and they are being cleared at an ever increasing rate. Currently, an area the size of a soccer field is lost every second. Rain forest is not the only type of habitat to have been lost. Temperate forest—the forest found in cooler regions where there are seasons—has disappeared along with grasslands and wetlands around the world.

## Deforestation

Tropical rain forest is found close to the equator where the temperature and rainfall is high all year round. These forests support an incredible diversity of animals and plants—as much as half of all the plant and animal species on Earth.

▲ Oil palm producers clear millions of acres (hectares) of rain forest to create farmland. Over 70 percent of the palm oil produced goes into foods such as chocolate and cream cheese.

◀ All Earth's great apes—gorillas, orangutans, chimpanzees, and bonobos—are critically endangered due to habitat loss, as are all Earth's tiger species.

8

## SOIL EROSION

Often, deforestation leads to soil erosion. When trees are felled, the soil is exposed to the sun, wind, and rain. Tropical soils are thin and are held in place by tree roots, while the leaves provide shelter. Without the trees, the heavy tropical rain falls on the unprotected soil and washes it away. Once the soil is washed away, or eroded, it has little value as it cannot be farmed.

Soils under rain forest trees usually lack nutrients. Even if the soil is farmed before it is washed away, it is soon exhausted by the crops. Once crops fail to grow, farmers abandon their fields and move to new areas to clear more forest. This short term gain is a waste of rainforest resources.

When eroded soil is washed away by heavy rains, it goes into streams and rivers. Often, there is so much soil that it clogs up the waterway and can lead to localized flooding. This means that settlements built in deforested areas are at risk of flooding.

▲ This land was once rain forest. When it rains, water runs down the slope, washing away the soil and forming gullies. Over time these gullies have got larger and now the land is useless.

Deforestation is the clearance of forests and it is happening in all the world's tropical rain forests. Rainforest trees provide high quality wood such as teak and mahogany, which is in demand for building and furniture making. Sometimes, the forests are bulldozed to make way for huge oil palm and rubber tree plantations, while small scale clearance takes place for growing crops.

In Central and South America, rain forest is cleared to make space for rearing beef cattle, in order to supply meat to North America and Europe.

Countries such as Brazil, in South America, and Indonesia, in Southeast Asia, have rapidly growing populations, so the people need space for new settlements.

The destruction of the rain forests is threatening the survival of thousands of animal species including large primates such as the chimpanzee and the orangutan.

## Global Forest Losses

The United Nations estimates that as much as 32 million acres (13 million ha) of forest are cleared around the world each year. Much of Europe's natural forest cover has already gone and in Northern Asia, in countries such as Russia and China, the huge conifer forests are being cleared at an alarming rate. The loss of these forests is threatening animals such as the Siberian tiger and Amur leopard.

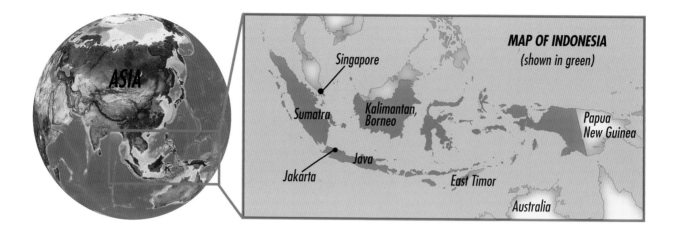

MAP OF INDONESIA
(shown in green)

ASIA

Singapore

Sumatra

Kalimantan, Borneo

Papua New Guinea

Java

Jakarta

East Timor

Australia

# Deforestation and Climate Change

Large-scale deforestation can even alter the climate in an area. The dark green canopy of a rain forest absorbs heat from the Sun and this heat is used to evaporate water from the surfaces of the leaves. The water returns to the atmosphere as water vapor, which then rises, cools, and condenses to form clouds. Eventually, the water falls to the ground again as rain. When large areas of rain forest are cleared, the water cycle is broken and then the area may get less rainfall. It might even suffer drought.

Trees take up carbon dioxide to use in photosynthesis, so fewer trees means that there is less uptake of carbon dioxide. Carbon dioxide is a greenhouse gas—one of the gases that trap heat around Earth, like a greenhouse traps heat, and causing global warming.

# Deforestation Caused by Migration

Indonesia is formed from a number of islands in Southeast Asia. The capital city, Jakarta, is located on Java, one of the most densely populated islands. To reduce the rapidly increasing population, the Indonesian government forced people to migrate to some of the other islands, especially East Timor, Papua New Guinea, and Kalimantan in Borneo. Between 1970 and 2000, around six million people were moved to the islands. There, the migrant families were each given a plot of forest to farm. Unfortunately, this has led to massive deforestation. In addition, the forests are being burned to make way for new palm oil and rubber plantations.

10

▼ ▶ *Top—A young orangutan plays with a worker at an orangutan rescue center. Large numbers of orangutans were killed, orphaned, or left homeless by the rainforest fires in Indonesia. Below—A migrant farmer uses fire to clear his land for farming on Kalimantan, Borneo. When forests are burnt, more carbon dioxide is released into the atmosphere because trees store carbon in their wood.*

## A Manmade Environmental Disaster

Many of the migrants from Java were resettled in forest areas of Kalimantan, Borneo, which were occupied by the Dayak. The Dayak live in small villages along rivers. They grow rice in small clearings, called swiddens, and collect other foods from the forest.

Some of the migrants from Java were part of a project, the Central Kalimantan Mega Project, which aimed to clear 2.5 million acres (one million ha) of swamp forest to create a major rice growing area. Experts warned that the soil was not suitable but the project went ahead. The forests were growing on a peat soil, which proved to be impossible to farm.

The rice-growing project was a complete disaster, and left vast cleared areas of land with no vegetation. As the peat dried out, the heat of the Sun caused it to catch on fire. The resulting fires smouldered in the ground for many months. The failure of the project left both the Dayak and migrants with no means to earn a living. During the dry season of 1997, massive fires burnt, partly from the cleared areas and also from illegal logging. Vast smoke clouds drifted over the whole region as far as Singapore and Jakarta, where thousands of people had to be treated for respiratory problems. Although the rice-growing project was abandoned, the annual fires continue today, adding carbon dioxide to the atmosphere. Now there are plans to flood the area and restore the original swamp forest.

▲ A tallgrass prairie habitat in midsummer in Illinois, U.S. The roots of prairie grasses extend deep into the soil. This allows the plants to obtain water in hot, dry summers.

▼ By 1936, the number of dirt storms had increased on the prairies in Oklahoma, Kansas, and Texas. Temperatures reached record highs and there was even an earthquake. Here, a vast dirt storm rolls over the landscape in Texas.

## Grasslands in Danger

Forests are not the only habitats cleared to make way for farmland. Earth's temperate grasslands, such as the prairies in North America and the steppes in Asia, occur in areas where the soil is deep and fertile. These grasslands have been plowed up to grow crops such as maize (corn), soya, and wheat, and have proved to be the most productive and fertile of all soils.

## The Dust Bowl

The economic depression of the 1920s and the massive unemployment that it caused resulted in many American families moving west in search of a better life. Many settled on the prairies, in states such as Oklahoma, Kansas, and Nebraska, where they plowed the grasslands and planted wheat. The climate of this region can be very variable. When there was plenty of rain the yields were high, but in drought years the crop would fail. During the 1930s the climate became particularly extreme. Winters were extremely cold with blizzards, while summer temperatures were hot and dry. Months of drought were followed by heavy rain, tornadoes, and flooding.

It was an incredibly difficult time for the farmers, desperate to grow food to survive. As one crop failed, they planted another, but nothing grew. The soil was dry and lacked cover. Strong winds blew away the soil, creating vast dirt storms that turned day into night, and made the air almost unbreathable. After the storms passed, everything was left covered in a thick layer of soil. It was an ecological disaster on a vast scale. People were forced from their homes and farms, and moved further west in search of new land to farm. The nickname "Okie" was given to the people that left the state of Oklahoma. There were hundreds of thousands of "Okies" and they settled in California and Oregon, often working as harvesters on farms.

▼ *This famous photograph of the poverty-stricken young migrant mother, Florence Owens Thompson, came to symbolize the hardship of the 1920s and 1930s for many Americans. The photo was taken by American photo-journalist Dorothea Lange as Florence and her young children camped out with other migrant workers who were pea picking in Nipomo, California.*

**JOURNEY STORIES**

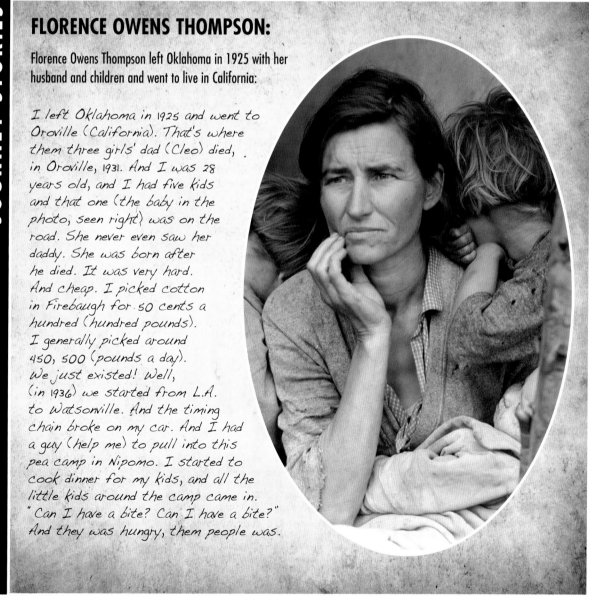

## FLORENCE OWENS THOMPSON:

Florence Owens Thompson left Oklahoma in 1925 with her husband and children and went to live in California:

I left Oklahoma in 1925 and went to Oroville (California). That's where them three girls' dad (Cleo) died, in Oroville, 1931. And I was 28 years old, and I had five kids and that one (the baby in the photo, seen right) was on the road. She never even saw her daddy. She was born after he died. It was very hard. And cheap. I picked cotton in Firebaugh for 50 cents a hundred (hundred pounds). I generally picked around 450, 500 (pounds a day). We just existed! Well, (in 1936) we started from L.A. to Watsonville. And the timing chain broke on my car. And I had a guy (help me) to pull into this pea camp in Nipomo. I started to cook dinner for my kids, and all the little kids around the camp came in. "Can I have a bite? Can I have a bite?" And they was hungry, them people was.

13

## BIOFUELS— GOOD OR BAD?

There is an important ongoing debate about whether biofuels such as ethanol and oil palm are good for the environment.

### BIOFUELS ARGUMENTS FOR:

• They are sustainable sources of fuel because the crop can be harvested and replanted.

• The plants release carbon dioxide when the fuel is burnt, but they take up carbon dioxide from the atmosphere as they grow. This means there is no loss or gain of carbon dioxide.

### BIOFUELS ARGUMENTS AGAINST:

• Large areas of land are needed to grow these crops. This means natural habitats such as grassland and rain forest are cleared to make space for them.

• When grassland is plowed up, the stored carbon in the soil is released which adds to the "greenhouse effect" causing global warming.

• Land that could be used for growing food is used for growing fuel.

▲ A field of corn grown to make ethanol. Eco-friendly, renewable biofuels are one way to reduce the use of non-renewable, greenhouse gas-producing oil-based fuels. Many people are concerned that wild habitats and the space to grow food will be lost to vast biofuel farms.

## A New Threat to the Prairies

Today, more than 90 percent of the natural tallgrass prairies in North America have disappeared. The remaining prairie has either been grazed by cattle or left as conservation areas. Now there are new concerns for the future of these remaining prairie lands. This time the threat comes from the biofuel, ethanol.

Ethanol is made from the sugar found in crops such as corn and wheat. The ethanol can be mixed with gasoline and used to fuel cars. Americans want to reduce their dependency on oil, and one way is to grow more corn for ethanol.

## Emergency Migrations

War and natural disasters can force people to flee their homes. Often, this happens quickly and unexpectedly with little time to prepare. In 2009, there were 15 million refugees worldwide. Refugees may settle in different locations, urban and rural. Some settle in refugee camps. Refugee camps are established by the government of the refugees' new country, with support from the United Nations Refugee Agency (UNHCR), other international humanitarian aid agencies, and/or local charitable organizations. The camps range from well run, established permanent camps to temporary camps with makeshift shelters—or no shelter at all—and no facilities such as running water and sanitation.

# The Environmental Effects of Refugee Migrations

Any huge and sudden arrival of refugees is likely to impact the environment. The impact they have depends on how their arrival is managed by the organizations, such as UNHCR, who support them. Refugees usually arrive at camps with only the possessions and food they can carry. In the urgency of an emergency situation, the initial priorities for both the refugees and the organizations that help them are safety, food, water, and shelter. In this emergency stage, protecting the environment is often low on the "to do" list! The amount of damage that a refugee camp can do to the environment at this stage depends on the numbers of refugees, the management of the camp, and the existing quality of the environment where the camp is located. Often, refugee camps are established on low-quality land where it is difficult to raise and graze animals.

The arrival of large numbers of refugees can anger the local population. They may be worried about damage to the environment, and the competition for resources such as firewood and locally available food. They may also resent the food aid, schools, and healthcare that some refugees in camps receive from aid agencies. Sometimes, refugee camps can become permanent fixtures where people live for decades. If this happens, refugees, aid agencies, and governments have to work to manage environmental damage and improve the living conditions in the camps.

▲ A young refugee gathers firewood from the area surrounding a refugee camp. The camp can be seen stretching for many acres (ha) into the distance.

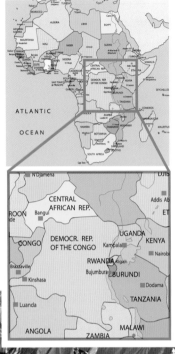

# People in Danger

In 1994, political upheavals in the central African country of Rwanda, led to the mass killings of Tutsi people and their sympathizers by Rwanda's other major ethnic group, the Hutu. In just 100 days, almost 750,000 people were brutally murdered. A further two million Tutsi and Hutu people fled into neighboring countries such as Burundi, Zaire (now called the Democratic Republic of Congo, DRC), Tanzania, and Uganda to avoid the attacks and reprisals.

More than 300,000 refugees streamed over the border from Rwanda into Tanzania and formed a vast refugee camp—so large that it immediately became Tanzania's second largest city. This influx of refugees and their makeshift "city" created endless problems for the Tanzanian government that was already trying to fight poverty amongst its own people. The Tanzanian people living in the area were mostly poor farmers

▼ *Often, refugee camps get larger, spreading out onto the surrounding land. With no drains for sewage, local water sources are soon polluted. Piles of rubbish build up, attracting pests such as rats. Under these conditions, diseases such as cholera and typhoid can spread rapidly. This refugee camp at Benako, Tanzania, Africa, was home to over 300,000 Rwandan refugees who fled fighting in their country in 1994.*

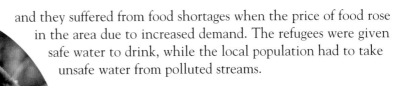

and they suffered from food shortages when the price of food rose in the area due to increased demand. The refugees were given safe water to drink, while the local population had to take unsafe water from polluted streams.

## The Environment in Danger

In Uganda, there were concerns that the Rwandan refugees would destroy nearby rain forests that were home to the endangered mountain gorilla. To help prevent this, wildlife charities, such as the Gorilla Organization, arranged a tree planting program to ensure a future supply of firewood, and helped set up livestock farming so that people did not go into the forest and kill the gorillas and other wild animals for food.

Over the last 20 years or more, the civil war in Somalia, in Africa, has led to more than 500,000 people fleeing across the borders to countries such as Ethiopia. By 2006, about 100,000 refugees were still living in camps in eastern Ethiopia. The area had suffered from deforestation and soil erosion, and water was in short supply. The UNHCR (United Nations Refugee Agency) tackled the massive problem of soil erosion by replanting trees on nearly 700 acres (280 ha) of bare land and terracing steep slopes to reduce water runoff. To improve the water supply, aid agencies set up water catchment basins to trap water during the rains. They also worked with the refugees to dig new wells and even built a long pipeline to bring in water from a highland area where water was plentiful.

▲ *There are fewer than 800 mountain gorillas left on Earth. Conservationists are working hard to protect them from hunters, and to protect the small pockets of rain forest where they live in Uganda, Rwanda, and the Democratic Republic of Congo.*

**JOURNEY STORIES**

## HABIBA:

Habiba lived in Mogadishu in war-torn Somalia. When a bomb landed next door and killed her neighbors in May 2009, Habiba decided it was time to flee. She rushed from the house, taking her eight-year-old disabled son Muse, and boarded a minibus bound for Kenya. Habiba didn't even wait for her husband to return from the market, so great was the danger. Habiba says,

*"In the last month, things have gotten worse in Mogadishu. People have been displaced, lost. You don't know where your neighbor is. When the fighting starts and there is gunfire and explosions in all directions, people are running, saying: Before it comes into my house, let me run."*

Habiba's journey took five long days, driving through the night. The journey ended at Dadaab, one of the world's largest refugee camps in Kenya. On arrival Habiba was given plastic sheets, soap, mats, and cans for water by the aid agencies working at the camp. Her new ration card allows her to collect food. Also she has found a wheelbarrow for Muse, so she doesn't have to carry him on her back anymore. Dadaab is terribly overcrowded, but Habiba has been able to share a shelter with a relative who has been at the camp for four years. Will Habiba return to her home? Habiba says,

*"Maya (no). Things won't get better. Maya, maya."*

▼ The Mississippi River snakes past the city of St. Louis, in Missouri, U.S. The city was founded in 1764 when French traders settled here to establish a trading center.

# CHAPTER THREE
# TAMING EARTH'S WATER

Throughout history many settlements have been built beside rivers because people need a constant supply of water. The river provided a year round supply of water, a source of food, and a means of transport. Often, river settlements have developed into major trading centers, such as Minneapolis and London.

## Controlling Rivers and Flooding

Living beside a river has its dangers, however. Water levels in rivers often change during the year, rising after heavy rains and snow melt, and falling during periods of dry weather.

When water levels rise and cause floods it can do incredible damage to settlements, so people are keen to control the flow of water in a river to reduce this risk. One of the easiest ways is to deepen and straighten the course of a river so its water flows straight out to sea. In some places, storm water can be diverted away from towns and cities onto low lying land near the river.

▲ In 2007, the city of Boston in the United Kingdom was identified as the place most at risk of flooding in the UK. Built on a flood plain, nearly 16,000 homes are at risk of flooding.

*◄ People escaping from a Mississippi River flood stand on top of a levee with their livestock in 1938.*

The low lying land beside a river is called the flood plain. This is land onto which flood waters spill during periods of heavy rain. Flood plains act as natural flood controls. However, in some densely populated places such as the United Kingdom and parts of China, people live on the flood plains and are at risk when the river floods.

Building on flood plains has other consequences. The flood plain may have important wildlife habitats such as wet meadows that are home to rare plants. When the river is altered to prevent flooding, wildlife habitats are altered too, and in some cases lost.

## The Mississippi River

The Mississippi River in North America floods regularly, causing great misery for the people living nearby. This great river, with the smaller rivers that join it, drains just over 40 percent of the United States plus a part of Canada. The river is like a huge funnel pushing water out into the Gulf of Mexico. In the 1800s, massive floods led to the setting up of the Mississippi River Commission in 1879 to improve flood defenses, and river navigation so that the river was safer and easier for shipping. To achieve this, the river's channel has been deepened. This means it can take more water and ships can travel further up the river. The river's banks have also been raised to form levees that contain floodwater and special floodways direct the water into storm basins.

*▼ Members of the National Guard construct an additional "back-up" sand bag levee next to the existing one as the Mississippi River threatens to flood Davenport, Iowa, in 2001.*

# Building Dams

People build dams across a river to create an artificial lake called a reservoir. Dams can be built from many different materials such as earth, rock, and concrete, which are laid across the narrowest part of the river. The dam stops the water from flowing downstream and forms a reservoir. Once a reservoir is in place, it is much easier to control the water flow in a river.

The water levels in the reservoir are controlled by sluice gates that allow some of the water to flow out. The store of water in the reservoir may be piped to settlements for drinking water or diverted along irrigation canals to water crops. The rest is released down the river. Dams help ship navigation too. Shipping can sail further upstream when the water levels are raised.

## Dams for Electricity

Dams are now being built to generate electricity in hydroelectric plants. The energy of falling water as it tumbles from the reservoir down pipes into the dam is converted into movement energy that spins turbine blades to generate electricity.

## The Three Gorges Dam

The world's largest hydroelectric dam is the Three Gorges Dam on the Yangtze River in China. Construction was completed in 2006 and the dam will be fully operational by 2012.

▲ *Yangtze River species such as the finless porpoise (seen here being checked by a conservationist) and the Yangtze River dolphin are critically endangered. There may only be a few Yangtze River dolphins left—some experts believe they are now extinct.*

◄ *There are many large hydroelectric plants around the world, including The Three Gorges Dam in China (seen here), the Hoover Dam on the Colorado River in the United States, and the Itaipu Dam on the Parana River between Paraguay and Brazil. The turbines of The Three Gorges Dam will generate just over ten percent of China's electricity.*

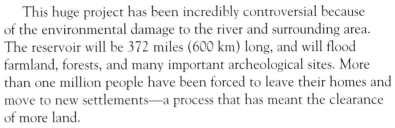

This huge project has been incredibly controversial because of the environmental damage to the river and surrounding area. The reservoir will be 372 miles (600 km) long, and will flood farmland, forests, and many important archeological sites. More than one million people have been forced to leave their homes and move to new settlements—a process that has meant the clearance of more land.

Although hydroelectricity is a clean and sustainable source of energy, the main reason for building the dam was to reduce flooding on the lower stretches of the river. The Yangtze floods were notorious, damaging major industrial cities such as Wuhan, Nanjing, and Shanghai, destroying homes and businesses, and ruining crops. The floods did serve a useful purpose, however. They carried away the industrial pollution from the industrial cities, keeping the Yangtze River relatively clean.

## Changes for the Worst

The building of dams and other changes to a river's course have an effect on the surrounding environment and wildlife.

Rivers entering a reservoir drop their silt, causing the reservoir to silt up over time. Below the dam, annual flooding is less common and the water carries less silt, which means less natural fertilization of farmland beside a river. Annual flooding was particularly important along the Nile River, in Africa. Annual flooding has been stopped by the building of the Aswan Dam in Egypt, in the 1960s. Now farmers along the Nile Valley below the dam have to spread artificial fertilizers on their fields. Often, wetlands below the dam disappear because the water levels are lowered and wetlands dry up. The Three Gorges Dam is now threatening the endangered Siberian crane that feeds on wetlands that will disappear under the reservoir.

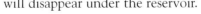

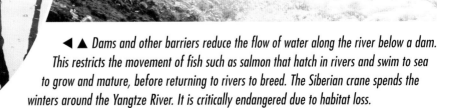

◀ ▲ *Dams and other barriers reduce the flow of water along the river below a dam. This restricts the movement of fish such as salmon that hatch in rivers and swim to sea to grow and mature, before returning to rivers to breed. The Siberian crane spends the winters around the Yangtze River. It is critically endangered due to habitat loss.*

21

## MAP OF THE GREAT LAKES IN NORTH AMERICA

## Lakeside Settlements

Lakes are also popular places for settlements. Some of the world's major cities are found beside lakes, such as Chicago that lies at the southern point of Lake Michigan. Geneva, Switzerland is another large lakeside city. It is situated next to Lake Geneva.

## The Great Lakes

The five Great Lakes in North America, Superior, Michigan, Huron, Erie, and Ontario hold 20 percent of Earth's fresh water, and support a great diversity of wildlife. But there is a problem—very little of the water is replenished. Each year, just one percent of the Great Lakes' total volume of water is replenished by rain and water draining into the lakes from the land and rivers. The same amount is lost through evaporation from the surface and water draining into the St. Lawrence River. For this reason, many people consider the water of the Great Lakes to be a non-renewable resource. Another problem is that any pollution caused by industry, sewage, or runoff from farmland remains in the lakes and builds up over time.

Around the lakes large cities have grown up. Major industry, such as steel and papermaking, and car manufacturing, as well as farmland also surrounds the lakes. Unfortunately, the Great Lakes have been used as dumping grounds for industrial waste and farm waste for centuries. Also, sewage and dirty storm water ends up in the lakes.

▼ The city of Chicago on the shore of Lake Michigan (seen here bottom left and right) is a major industrial and residential area. More than 40 million people live in the Great Lakes Basin. A basin is a shallow depression in the surface of Earth with a lake lying at the bottom.

## Keeping the Great Lakes Clean

Today, there are strict controls to ensure that industry cleans its waste water before it enters the Great Lakes. However, one problem area that needs to be tackled is storm water. Heavy rain sometimes overloads the drains in the cities surrounding the lakes. Storm water pours into the lakes carrying with it the debris, such as garbage and oil, from the cities' streets. Sewage may end up in the lakes as some of the treatment plants in the area are overloaded. Raw sewage contains bacteria and a lot of nutrients and when these enter the water they upset the natural balance, often reducing the oxygen levels and killing fish and other lake animals. Today, new landscaping projects are aiming to reduce this storm water runoff. Natural habitats, such as forests and wetlands, can hold and filter storm water, releasing it gradually. Now there are plans around the Great Lakes to restore woodland, grassland, and wetland habitats that were destroyed when the cities and industrial areas were built.

## The Threat of Rising Sea Levels

Coasts are ever-changing landscapes. The constant battering by the waves causes cliffs to crumble and beaches to be washed away. While some coastlines are retreating, others are growing as the tides bring in the sand from other beaches. Sea levels have been rising slowly since the end of

◄ *A view of mangrove roots under water. Scientific research has shown that up to 90 percent of a wave's energy can be absorbed by mangroves, helping to protect coasts from erosion.*

## MANGROVE SWAMPS

Mangrove swamps are found along tropical coastlines, especially near the mouth of a river. They are important for wildlife, especially fish, but more importantly they protect the coast. Unfortunately, mangrove swamps have been cleared to make way for new ports, industrial centers, marinas, and hotel complexes. This leaves the coast more vulnerable to storm damage. In the Indonesian tsunami of 2004, coasts with mangrove swamps suffered far less damage than those with none. Now many countries have programs to re-establish their mangrove swamps.

the last Ice Age, about 11,000 years ago, and this has increased coastal erosion in some places. Manmade global warming is making matters worse, however. The polar ice caps and glaciers are melting and the seawater itself is expanding as it gets warmer. In some places, the sea level has risen by 10 inches (25 cm) over the last 100 years. As sea levels rise, the coastal erosion increases threatening our coastal settlements. As many as 350,000 homes in the United States lie within 490 feet (150 m) of the shore. Each year about 1,500 of them fall into the ocean because of coastal erosion.

It's not just human settlements that are threatened by flooding: valuable wildlife habitats such as low lying salt marshes and coastal wetlands are also in danger. In Louisiana, an area of wetland the size of a football field is lost under the sea every 30 minutes!

## Coastal Defenses

So what do we do? Historically, people abandoned settlements that got too close to the coast. Today, this is not always possible, so vulnerable coasts are protected by barriers such as groynes (below bottom left) and rock piles. Scientists are also considering the possibility of building barrier islands off of coasts to weaken the waves before they hit the coast.

## Holding Back the Waters

Much of the Netherlands lies below sea level. The lowest point in the country is 23 feet (7 m) below sea level. About 1,000 years ago, when sea levels were lower, people settled in this region and started to farm the rich soils. As the sea level rose, it raised the level of rivers in the area so the people built banks called dikes to stop floodwater from rivers pouring over the land.

As the population grew, the Dutch people started to reclaim land from the sea to provide more farmland. They built new dikes and used windmills to pump water from the fields. The sea level continued to rise, so the

◄ *Clockwise from top left — a house balances on the edge of an eroded cliff; erosion on the Pacific coast of U.S.; a groyne defense; a defensive sea wall and rock pile.*

24

◀ At the North Pole, the Arctic Ocean around the polar ice cap freezes and joins the ice cap to Canada and other Arctic coasts during the winter. Polar bears leave the land and hunt for seals on the frozen ocean during this time. Now, the ice cap is melting and the amount of sea ice is decreasing due to global warming. The ocean freezes for a shorter period of time each year, too. The loss of their hunting grounds and the shortening of their hunting season is endangering the polar bears' future survival.

dikes got taller and taller. The rivers were straightened and dredged so they could carry more water, and channels were built to carry away floodwater.

## When Nature Can't be Tamed

In 1953, a storm surge along the North Sea coast caused massive devastation. A storm surge is when strong winds ahead of a storm push on the water creating huge tides that flood the land. Much of the low lying land was flooded and 1,800 people were killed.

Following the disaster, the government devised the Delta Plan, which involved reinforcing coastal defenses and closing off the estuaries with huge dams. However, this slowed down the flow of water along the rivers, and in times of heavy rain, the people couldn't stop the rivers from flooding. So, the dikes were raised again.

With sea levels still rising today, the country's latest plans involve the building of shallow basins beside some of the rivers where floodwater can be diverted.

▲ Here, a road and wind farm have been constructed along the top of a dike in the Netherlands.

▼ In newly industrialized countries, such as India and China, cities are growing fast. Here, construction is completed on the Shanghai World Financial Center in Shanghai, China.

# CHAPTER FOUR

# URBANIZATION

**In the early 1900s, just 13 percent of the world's population lived in towns and cities. Since then, the migration of people from rural areas has caused the urban areas, or cities, to grow. By 2008, about half the world's people lived in urban areas. We call this migration of people to cities and the subsequent growth of those cities urbanization.**

## Why Do Cities Grow?

People migrate to cities for many reasons. Two hundred years ago in Europe, the Industrial Revolution—a period in time when technology advanced significantly—led to a stream of people moving from rural areas to cities in search of a better life. A similar pattern followed in North America. The mechanization of agriculture and improvements in farming methods made many agricultural workers jobless. At the same time, advances in steam technology allowed the development of machines capable of mass production. Factories that mass-produced textiles sprung up, both in Europe and the eastern United States. Soon, large factory towns grew up to house the workers needed to fill the new urban, factory jobs. Today, this pattern of urbanization is repeating itself in the less economically developed countries of Asia and Africa.

## The Pull of Urban Life

Today, people in developing countries are attracted to cities because of the chance of better jobs. Cities usually have better schooling and health care, too. Cities in developing countries often give people more chance of improving their standards of living compared with the hard work of living off the land. In wealthier countries, cities offer easier commutes, a better choice of schools and hospitals, and entertainment such as restaurants, cinemas, theaters, and museums.

## Growing Environmental Pressures

A growing city puts pressure on the environment. The city expands into the suburbs, and beyond, as more housing is needed, and industrial centers spring up. This results in the loss of green spaces and wildlife habitats.

Cities need a lot of water each day and this is drawn from nearby rivers and wells. Toronto, Canada, for example, uses an average of 300 million gallons (1,136 million liters) of water every day. Toronto lies on Lake Ontario, so the water is taken from the lake. One way to supply a city's water needs is to dam a river, build a reservoir, and pipe the water to the city. In New York, the city's eight million residents get water from 19 reservoirs and three lakes.

Many cities rely on water from wells, for example in Ho Chi Minh City in Vietnam there are more than 300,000 wells, many dug by residents. More water is being drawn from the ground than is replenished by rain, however, so the water levels have dropped by up to 33 feet (10 m). Now the wells have to reach down as much as 490 feet (150 m) to find water. The water quality is falling too, due to pollution from the city.

## Waste Mountains

Traditionally, waste from cities is either burnt or transported to local landfills. Now, the volumes of waste are so great that the landfills are filling up and cities are forced to transport their waste further. In Toronto, the last landfill was filled in 2002 so the city's waste is taken by water to landfills in Michigan, U.S. The city of New York produces about 12,000 tons (12,000 tonnes) of garbage a day which is transported out of the city in trucks and by barge. The city is finding it difficult to persuade neighboring states to accept its waste, though. The problem is also occurring in fast-growing cities in countries such as China. Waste in China is burnt, composted, put in landfills, or simply dumped on bare land.

▲ *The artificial city environment is very different from the surrounding area and it may even influence the climate. The presence of people, buildings, industry, and cars kicks out heat, so a city is usually several degrees warmer than the surrounding area. Here, the capital city of Japan, Tokyo, spreads for many miles into the distance. Tokyo has the largest population of any city in the world—over 35 million people live in the city center and suburbs.*

## Suburbanization

As a city grows, it becomes wealthier and the cost of housing rises. Expensive housing, road congestion, and the high density of people causes many city residents to relocate to the suburbs— the residential areas around a city, where housing is cheaper. The growth of suburbs is known as suburbanization. Shopping malls, industrial parks, and offices are built in the suburbs and gradually the city sprawls onto land lying beyond its fringe, causing more habitat loss. Some cities recognize the need to limit this expansion. They establish green belts or green space around the city on which development cannot take place. This idea was first proposed in the United Kingdom during the 1930s when a green belt was established around London. Now, 13 percent of land in the United Kingdom is protected as green belt.

## Sprawling Slums

In many countries, migrants to cities cannot afford housing in the city. They may even arrive only to find they are unable to obtain work. This leads to the development of slums or "shantytowns" on the outskirts of cities. Here, there is extreme poverty. There will also be no infrastructure such as tarmac roads, water supplies, sewage systems, waste collections, or schools and medical facilities. Sometimes, these shanty towns are large enough to be called sub-cities. Not surprisingly, shantytowns damage the environment. It's not just the loss of habitat when people build their shacks, but the lack of drains and sewage treatment means that raw sewage pours into local waterways where it kills fish and other animals. The polluted water soaks into the ground where it contaminates the water supply to wells.

▲ In South Africa, the huge, sprawling slum, or township, of Soweto (seen above) exists just outside of Johannesburg. Soweto and other South African townships sprung up to house the thousands of workers who were transported from their homelands hundreds of miles away to work in the gold mines.

## The Industrialization and Urbanization of China

Urbanization is growing at a very fast rate in China. It's taken just over 20 years for the urban population to grow from just 18 percent to almost 40 percent—by 2035 it is estimated 70 percent of the people in China will be living in cities.

Until the 1970s, there was little urbanization in China because the central government had a tight control over migration. A change in government leadership and policy led to a relaxation of the rules, which allowed people to move where they wished. Improvements in agriculture meant fewer farm workers were needed. The widespread unemployment in rural areas and rapid industrialization in growth centers, particularly around Beijing and Shanghai, led to a massive migration.

▲ ▶ *Migrant workers sort plastic bottles at a recycling center on the outskirts of Beijing, China. Garbage is becoming a huge problem for China. It is estimated that by 2020, the country will be dealing with a garbage pile up of 400 million tons (400 million tonnes). Right—Poverty-stricken families live on the edge of a polluted and garbage strewn stream in the slums of Bangalore, India.*

The expansion of the cities and improvements in the standard of living for many millions of Chinese people has meant that more people own cars. Traffic congestion is commonplace in major cities and this creates air pollution. People can also afford more electrical goods such as refrigerators, televisions, and computers, so there are more factories and a greater demand for raw materials such as oil and steel. All this growth has led to an increased demand for electricity, so hundreds of new power stations have been built.

The carbon dioxide emissions from these power stations, cars, and factories is contributing to climate change. By 2006, China overtook the United States as the world's largest producer of carbon dioxide.

# CHAPTER FIVE

# GETTING AROUND

Hundreds of years ago, people rarely traveled beyond their village. Today, we think nothing of traveling to the other side of the world just for a vacation. Every day, millions of people commute to work or school—some travel many miles. All these daily and short-term migrations are having a serious effect on the environment.

## More and More Roads

As cities grow, so does the infrastructure needed to support them such as roads, railways, and airports. In turn, the increase in infrastructure causes more damage to the environment.

▲ New road construction underway in Chongqing, China. The area's economy is growing fast—especially its automobile industry, which manufactured one million cars in 2007.

◀ In some major cities, the traffic never stops! Cars choke the roads, pumping carbon emissions and pollution into the atmosphere, 24 hours a day, 365 days a year.

▲ *Researchers found that rain forests that already had roads and some deforestation were eight times more likely to be occupied by new farmers than untouched forest.*

In densely populated countries such as the United Kingdom, road expansion has caused problems. New road plans have been highly unpopular because of the damage to the environment. In the United Kingdom, controversial plans for a new bypass to reduce congestion around the town of Newbury upset conservationists. The new route passed through woodlands, and nature reserves, one of which was home to a rare species of snail. Despite the numerous objections the new road was built.

New roads can lead to further environmental damage. Not only does the traffic pollute the atmosphere, but the new road is often followed by further development in the area. In Brazil, roads have been formed through rain forests to provide access for logging trucks that carry away timber. Unfortunately, these new roads have made it easier for other people to access the forests, which leads to further deforestation.

# FOCUS ON:

## ROAD PROTESTORS

In 1993, the UK government announced plans for a new bypass near the city of Bath, UK. The bypass was one of the many road plans in their master plan to build a network of major roads. This road would drive through Solsbury Hill, an ancient hill fort in an area of unspoiled countryside on the outskirts of the city—also the hill that inspired Peter Gabriel's 1977 song. During the winter of 1993-1994, protesters came from all over the United Kingdom. They set up a camp and tree houses to try to stop the bulldozers. The protesters remained for more than six months but eventually they were forcibly removed and the new road was built. This protest marked a turning point. It was the first of many road protests and involved ordinary people from all walks of life protecting their environment. The Solsbury Hill protest and the other road protests that came after caused the UK government to remove 300 road plans from their master plan.

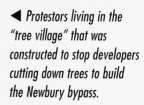

◀ *Protestors living in the "tree village" that was constructed to stop developers cutting down trees to build the Newbury bypass.*

## THE QINGHAI-TIBET RAILWAY

In China, a new 620-mile-long (1,000-km-long) railway has been built across the Himalayan Mountains linking Lhasa in Tibet with the rest of China. It was a major feat of engineering. Before the railway, the only way into Tibet was by air or by road—a journey that took three days driving along dangerous mountain roads where accidents were commonplace.

This railway could change Tibet forever, attracting migrants and tourists from other parts of China. All of a sudden there is a lot of money in Lhasa, new buildings are appearing and the traditional Tibetan way of life is under threat. Conservationists worry that the new railway, which destroyed fragile mountain habitats, will threaten the migration routes of the rare Tibetan antelope.

*"It's a good idea. It'll make it easier for us to take our wool down to the market. At the moment we have to hire a truck to come up here, but with a train it'll be cheaper and easier."*

Tibetan herder with wool to sell in China

*"Once damaged, it is extremely difficult to reverse. Integrating the needs of local development with conserving Tibet's biodiversity is in need of urgent attention."*

Dawa Tsering, WWF China, talking about the need to protect the fragile ecosystems of the Tibetan plateau

▲▼ *The recently completed Qinghai-Tibet railway between China and Tibet crosses the Himalayan feeding and migration grounds of the endangered Tibetan antelope (a calf is pictured below). Special animal migration passages have been constructed beneath the railway.*

## Daily Migrations

A good road network causes other problems. When road travel is made easier, people are able to drive longer distances to work. This leads to more traffic, more fuel being used, and more carbon dioxide emissions.

More cars can mean more parking lots. These are often built on land on the outskirts of cities increasing the amount of green space destroyed by the city.

## Air Travel on the Increase

Each month, there are about 2.5 million flights around the world and this number is increasing by about five percent a year—that's an extra 100,000 flights a month. Some estimates suggest that the number of flights within Europe will triple by 2030. There is also a boom in air travel in countries such as China and India due to greater wealth, and poor ground transport systems.

Air travel has made long commutes much easier and often more economical, especially with the arrival of low cost airlines. In North America, many people hop on a plane to travel to another part of the country in much the same way as people take buses in other parts of the world.

▲ Nitrous oxide from aircraft exhaust emissions is a greenhouse gas. It will destroy ozone at high altitude in the ozone layer, and this allows more ultraviolet light to reach the Earth's surface. High levels of ultraviolet light have been linked to skin cancer and eye problems.

▼ An airport soon attracts other businesses too, so industrial parks spring up. This creates jobs and wealth, but the environment is damaged by the creation of the industrial park, and by the workers commuting to their jobs each day. Is this an economic hub, or a huge scar on the landscape? From the air it's possible to see the vast area covered by an airport (Toronto Pearson Airport in Canada) and its surrounding industrial areas.

# Aircraft Carbon Emissions

Air travel is the method of transport that contributes most to global warming. It produces about three percent of the world's carbon dioxide emissions. Aircraft engines produce an exhaust that contains several gases, including carbon dioxide and nitrous oxide. These emissions are particularly problematic because they have a much greater effect at altitude, compared with similar emissions at ground level. For example, 1 ton (1 tonne) of carbon dioxide emitted by an aircraft at altitude is as damaging as 2.5 tons (2.5 tonnes) of carbon dioxide produced on the ground.

Controlling aircraft emissions is tricky as they are created by international activities and are exempt from international environmental treaties, or agreements, such as the Kyoto Treaty. There is no easy fix for this problem. The only way to reduce aircraft emissions is to cut down on the number of flights. This could be achieved by taxing air travel heavily and by using cleaner and more efficient planes that carry more people for the same amount of fuel. It can also be achieved by educating people to cut the number of flights they take—especially short flights where alternative transport methods are available, such as trains.

# Airports and Environmental Damage

Many airports are built just outside a city so that travelers can reach the city center quickly. Airports spread over large areas— for example, Charles De Gaulle outside Paris, France, covers more than 7,400 acres (3,000 ha)—causing extensive loss of wildlife habitat and green spaces. Airports are also served by road and rail links which take up more space.

## THE HEATHROW AIRPORT THIRD RUNWAY DEBATE

The proposed development of a third runway at Heathrow Airport in London has created a heated debate that includes many different viewpoints on how we travel, where people live and work, conservation issues, and much more.

*"This decision opens the door to Heathrow becoming a truly world class hub airport, and to the UK maintaining the direct connections to the rest of the world on which our prosperity depends."*
**Colin Matthews, Chief Executive of BAA (the owners of Heathrow Airport)**

*"This package (the environmental conditions linked to the planning consents) will do very little to reduce the huge environmental impact of an expanded Heathrow, which will now become the single biggest emitter of carbon dioxide in the country."*
**John Sauven, Director of Greenpeace**

*"Air transport will continue to play an important role in our lives in the 21st century, but massive questions remain over exactly what that role should be, and what proportion of carbon emissions we want to devote to it as opposed to our homes, food production, and other forms of travel."*
**Hugh Raven, Sustainable Development Commission in the UK**

▲ Protestors and members of the environmental political party, the Green Party, campaign against the planned third runway at Heathrow airport, near London, in May 2008.

## The Expansion of Heathrow Airport

As air travel becomes even more popular, there is pressure on the world's leading airports to expand by building new terminals and runways. Heathrow Airport, near London, is one of the world's busiest airports. Heathrow has only two runways and now there are plans to build a third. In addition, public transport to the airport will be improved creating a major transport hub with 60,000 new jobs, both in train and bus transport as well as travel-related businesses.

The UK government and the developers who will build the new runway have made promises that only the latest aircraft with low noise and emissions will be allowed to use the new runway to minimize pollution. However, the development requires the demolition of about 700 homes, including a whole village and a school. Also in the way are water meadows, which are home to rare plants that are found in few other sites in the United Kingdom. Thousands of people will be affected and many will have to move to other parts of London or further.

## Vacation Travel

Fifty years ago people tended to vacation within their own country. The arrival of commercial, affordable air travel opened up a wide selection of new destinations, including faraway vacation resorts in Africa and Asia.

In recent years, cheap tickets have encouraged even more people to take short breaks overseas, or even to buy vacation homes in foreign countries. But there is an environmental cost. Large numbers of tourist migrants can have an impact on the local environment in a town, or in a rural or coastal area. More hotels and resorts are built as a tourist destination becomes popular to accommodate the extra vacationers, and new airports and improved road systems are needed. Remote, unspoiled islands are soon ruined by thousands of vacationers on large capacity planes.

Tourists do bring in money and create jobs in an area, but they also put extra demands on resources, such as water supplies, which may already be in short supply during the summer months.

▼ *A diver explores corals off the Red Sea coast. The corals have suffered damage due to a rise in the number of divers visiting the reefs, and the building of tourist resorts on the nearby coast.*

## FOCUS ON:

## PARADISE LOST

In the early 1980s, Sharm El Sheikh was a sleepy fishing village on the Red Sea coast of Egypt. The area was close to the pristine coral reefs of the Red Sea. It was soon recognized as a top scuba-diving site and there was a rush to build new vacation resorts. The coral reefs were soon damaged.

The towns of Sharm El Sheikh and nearby Hurghada virtually doubled in size every few years. Now, three million people visit the Egyptian Red Sea coast every year. The coastline has been altered by the building of marinas and new resorts. Many hotels have their own mini-sewage treatment plants that can get overloaded and discharge inadequately treated sewage into the Red Sea.

One cause of damage to the reefs was the rise in diver numbers—at times there were as many as 4,000 divers in the water each day. Dive boats damaged the reefs by banging on the corals. Divers touched the corals and pulled off pieces as souvenirs. Sand and silt from building sites washed into the water and smothered the corals. Desalination plants—which change salt water into fresh water—have been built because fresh water is in short supply in this desert region. The plants empty their extremely salty waste into the ocean, damaging the reefs. Sadly, the damage continues.

# CHAPTER SIX

# A VERY CROWDED PLANET

Each year, the world's population grows by around 75 million. That's about 200,000 people every day—the size of a city! Currently, two babies are born for every person who dies.

## Why is the World's Population Increasing?

The population increase is due mostly to the decline in death rates in developing countries such India, Pakistan, and many African nations. Improved public health care and disease prevention, such as vaccination programs, in developing countries means infant mortality rates, or the

◀ ▲ *By the year 2013, there will be seven billion people on Earth. As the population continues to grow, how much land will be swallowed up to provide homes and places to grow food?*

number of babies that die in their first year, are dropping and people are now living longer, healthier lives. Overall, though, the world's population is young. One in every five people is between the ages of 15 and 24, and most of these young people live in developing countries, especially in Africa.

## Fifteen Billion People

Population increase is not the same all over the world. Population growth is slowing down in Europe and North America, but it is increasing in China, India, and in Africa. For example, China's population is predicted to reach 1.43 billion within the next 40 years—up from 1.3 billion in 2009. By the year 2050, experts have predicted that the global population could be as much as 15 billion.

## More People, More Climate Change

This rapid rise in the world's population means more environmental damage. The human activity with the greatest impact on the environment is the burning of fuel—wood and especially fossil fuels. The increase in population numbers will mean more carbon dioxide released into the atmosphere and a further increase in global warming. As global warming increases, it will cause more climate change leading to extreme weather such as drought, flood, and storms becoming more common. More people on Earth will also mean more pollution entering the world's oceans and waterways, and more waste buried in the ground.

▲ *Many African children die from preventable diseases. Save The Children are vaccinating children against measles and distributing mosquito nets to families to protect them from mosquito bites that spread malaria.*

## More People, More Resources Needed

Fossil fuels are vitally important to our modern lives. We depend upon the energy they create for transport, electricity, and the production and manufacturing of the food we eat, the clothes we wear, and the materials from which we build our homes. As the world's population grows, our energy needs will grow, too. This is a problem with two parts: first the types of energy we use—fossil fuels—are causing climate change; second, fossil fuels are non-renewable—they are running out!

Other resources such as timber and water will also be under pressure as the world's population grows. The need for space to build homes and grow food will increase, too, which could lead to more deforestation and loss of green spaces.

So, how will we cope with twice as many people on the planet? How will we ensure we have enough resources, while not damaging our planet even more than we already have?

# CHAPTER SEVEN

# TOMORROW'S ECO-FRIENDLY SETTLEMENTS

With the world's population on course to hit 15 billion people by the middle of this century, space for new settlements and the need for resources to serve those settlements will grow. Careful planning and design will be needed to make sure tomorrow's settlements minimize damage to the environment.

## Green Cities Around the World

Curitiba in Brazil is probably the world's best example of a green city. Its mass transit system moves 70 percent of the population, and its innovative waste system allows residents to swap scrap metals, glass,

and rags for locally produced food.

Treasure Island is not a remote tropical island, but a 988 acre (400 ha) manmade island in the middle of San Francisco Bay that was built in 1939. It is the site of one of the greenest developments in the United States. There will be sustainable homes for 13,000 residents and plenty of wind turbines and solar panels on all the roofs, so the island is self-sufficient in energy. An organic farm will supply the residents with locally grown food. Sewage and dirty water is treated naturally using a large artificial wetland, so that all the waste water from the island is safe to enter San Francisco Bay.

## Green City Design

A green city of the future will achieve a massive reduction in the use of fossil fuels, or will have eliminated them all together. The electricity will come from a renewable energy source. The buildings will be constructed from renewable materials such as wood. Rainwater will be collected all around the city to be used in toilets and for irrigating gardens and parks. Waste will be minimized by recycling, composting food and green waste, and burning the rest in waste-to-energy power plants. Instead of sewage treatment plants, the sewage and dirty water may be treated naturally using reed beds or artificial wetlands. In a reed bed, the dirty water is allowed to flow slowly around the roots of the reeds, which remove the harmful materials from the water.

◄ *In an eco-friendly city there will be green spaces with trees and pedestrian friendly streets to encourage walking. There will be a good public transport network so car ownership becomes unnecessary. Finally, the green city will have mixed neighborhoods where people can live, shop, and work in the same area so there is less need to commute.*

◄ *Incorporating trees and plants in city designs is important, such as planting trees along roads, and planting green roofs and walls (seen left and on page 38).*

## GREEN ROOFS

Space is lacking in most cities, but there are many buildings with roofs that are perfect for creating gardens, wildlife areas, and even for growing vegetables. Rooftop gardens make a city look more attractive, bring birds and other wildlife into the city, and the plants help to take up the carbon dioxide caused by cars and the city's activities. The thick layer of soil and plants provides insulation by reducing the loss of heat from the top of a building, cutting the building's energy usage.

Rooftop gardens are also one way that stormwater runoff from buildings can be reduced. The soil holds water and the plants will use it for irrigation. This stops the runoff flooding drains and potentially entering rivers and lakes.

In some cities, such as New York, there are even rooftop farms on large industrial buildings. Rooftop farms enable a city to become far more self-sufficient in fresh food.

# Where Will We Build Green Cities?

In the future, planners will have to look carefully at where new cities can be built to minimize damage to the environment. In densely populated countries such as the Netherlands and the United Kingdom, there are few places left that are suitable for building new settlements. Flood plains are dangerous places to build. Most of the remaining wildlife habitats in Europe are protected, so that leaves farmland. But farmland will be needed in the future to grow food. So where do planners look? They need sites where there are good transport links, a source of renewable energy, fresh water, and farmland to supply the new city with food. A greener option is to avoid building new towns and cities altogether, by making better use of the space in existing cities. Old industrial sites and other derelict land can be used to build new homes. Housing density will have to be higher to accommodate more people, so it is likely that the greener cities will have eco-skyscrapers. The Pearl River Tower in Guangzhou, China, will be one of the most energy efficient skyscrapers ever built, with wind turbines, solar panels, and water-cooled ceilings. It will reduce its energy consumption by half compared with similar buildings.

▲ This bus in London is powered by hydrogen fuel cells that produce no pollution and zero carbon emissions. The hydrogen is stored in cylinders on top of the bus. The hydrogen reacts with oxygen to produce energy, which powers the bus's motor, and water vapor, which is the system's only emission.

## Reducing Congestion

One effective way to make a city more eco-friendly is to reduce the number of vehicles on the city's roads. This can be achieved in many ways, but the key is setting up a good mass transit system, which offers more comfortable, convenient, and cheaper travel compared with taking the car. Another requirement is that people can access the transport system by foot or bike, so they do not have to use their cars.

New York City's mass transit system of over and underground transport links is used by 4.5 million people a day. It is so effective that half the people living in the city do not own a car. In London, a new fleet of pollution-free buses has been introduced that are powered by fuel cells.

Electricity is the most widely used form of energy. A report for the Organisation for Economic Co-operation and Development (OECD), estimated that between 2002 and the year 2030, global demand would double. This will be partly due to the increasing industrialization of countries such as China and India.

Currently, fossil fuels and nuclear energy are responsible for generating about 80 percent of the world's electricity. Hydroelectric supplies a further 16 percent and the remaining four percent comes from renewables such as wind and solar power, wave power, geothermal energy—heat from the ground—and biomass—gas created by rotting waste and plants.

So can renewable energy sources supply all the world's future electricity needs?

## FOCUS ON:

### GREEN CARS

Today, most cars are fueled by gasoline or diesel. But with fossil fuels running out, the car of the future will be very different. Currently, the most popular green cars are the hybrid cars, such as the Toyota Prius, that are powered by an electric motor in cities but can switch to a fuel-efficient engine for longer journeys. However, they still use fossil fuels.

The future car will probably be all electric or be powered by a fuel cell. Electric cars are already on our roads. They have a battery and an electric motor. They can't go as fast as traditional cars, but that does not matter on congested city streets. The downside is the need to recharge the battery while it is parked. Engineers are working on new designs of battery that allow an electric car to travel for further before they need to be recharged.

Even better is the car powered by a fuel cell. Fuel cells run on clean fuels such as hydrogen and the only waste produced is water.

◀ *The electricity to run an electric car is often generated by burning fossil fuels, so the ideal situation is for electric cars to use renewable energy such as solar power (seen here).*

## WIND FARMS

Wind farms are a source of clean, renewable energy, which many people think are an interesting addition to the countryside.

Others feel that wind farms scar the landscape and destroy natural habitats. Some conservationists worry that birds will fly into the blades and that large wind farms may disorientate migrating birds and throw them off course.

*To generate the same amount of electricity as today's U.S. wind turbine fleet of 21,000 MW would require burning 30.4 million tons (tonnes) of coal—a line of 10-ton trucks over 11,500 miles (18,500 km) long—or 21 million barrels of oil each year.*

**American Wind Energy Association**

*That land belongs to the people for recreation, hiking, scenic sightseeing, and other traditional uses. It should not be given to power companies.*

**County Commissioner Lamont Pagenhardt in 2008 on proposals to build a wind farm on 400 acres (162 ha) of state forest in Maryland, U.S.**

*The RSPB does not object routinely to all wind turbine sites, but does lodge planning objections against those that pose a risk to migrating birds or vulnerable populations of birds and habitats.*

**Royal Society for the Protection of Birds (RSPB), UK, 2008**

Scientists have calculated that there is more than enough solar and wind energy available, it's just a question of harnessing it. The windiest places tend to be far from cities and the windiest times of year do not always coincide with peak energy demand.

Renewable energy sources may become the main supplier of electricity in less developed countries that lack their own fossil fuel supplies and do not have a high energy requirement, such as Bangladesh and Tanzania. Small scale renewable programs can supply electricity to remote communities that are beyond the reach of traditional power lines. For example, a collection of solar panels is sufficient to power a village.

In developed countries, such as the United States and United Kingdom, it is unlikely that renewables will be able to meet demand, at least not in the short term. As technology improves, however, so will our ability to make better use of renewable energy, while reducing dependency on fossil fuels and cutting carbon emissions.

## A Fossil Fuel Free Future?

Iceland is planning to be the world's first fossil fuel-free economy by 2050. About two-thirds of Iceland's current energy needs comes from hydroelectric power, and geothermal energy that uses heat from the ground. Geothermal energy is readily available across Iceland because the island is volcanic, and there are hot rocks just below the surface.

At the center of Iceland's future plans is hydrogen. Hydrogen gas is made by passing an electric current through water. At the moment, most of the world's hydrogen is made using electricity

◄ *Many people do not want wind farms near their homes. They do not want to live with the constant whooshing noise of the turbines and flickering lights that are created as the spinning blades catch the Sun. This has led to anti-wind farm protests in some areas.*

from fossil fuel-powered power stations. However, in countries such as Iceland, the renewable energy sources could be used to make hydrogen to power fuel cells. A fuel cell is a bit like a battery. It generates electricity by reacting two chemicals together, for example hydrogen and oxygen. Within the next few decades fuel cells will be used in Iceland to power all the country's vehicles, its fishing fleet, and to generate electricity in buildings.

## Our Changing Planet

For thousands of years, humans have moved around Earth, building settlements and changing the face of the planet to suit their needs. Today, we understand that many of the changes we have made have damaged and will continue to damage Earth unless we change the way we live and use Earth's resources. The good news is that we have the ideas and much of the technology we need to live in a more environmentally friendly and sustainable way. Now, we must begin to change our planet for the better.

▼ *Iceland's five geothermal power stations provide more than 25 percent of the country's electricity and almost 90 percent of the hot water and heating in homes.*

*"Only after the last tree has been cut down. Only after the last river has been poisoned. Only after the last fish has been eaten. Only then will you find that money cannot be eaten."*
Cree Indian saying

# GLOSSARY

**atmosphere** The layer of gases that surrounds Earth

**biodiversity** The shortened term for "biological diversity." It means every living thing on Earth—microorganisms, animals, humans, and plants

**biofuel** A renewable fuel that is formed from recently grown plant material such as straw, willow, or animal wastes such as manure

**carbon emissions** The release of carbon dioxide, or $CO_2$, into the atmosphere as a result of burning fossil fuels such as coal and oil. $CO_2$ is a greenhouse gas that can, when present at certain levels, pollute Earth's atmosphere and other resources and cause harm to plant and animal life

**CFCs (chlorofluorocarbons)** Chemicals that were used in aerosols and refrigerators, now known to damage the ozone layer and to act as a greenhouse gas

**commute** A regular journey between home and work

**congestion** Overcrowding of streets caused by too many vehicles. This causes slower speeds and traffic jams

**conservation** The preservation and protection of habitats, and the animals and plants that live in them, through careful management

**deforestation** The clearance of forests

**drought** A period of lower-than-normal rainfall over a given timespan. Droughts can often lead to the deaths of large numbers of people, animals, and plants as water in a region dries up

**eco-skyscraper** A skyscraper built using environmentally friendly and sustainable materials, and designed to reduce its use of energy and resources such as water

**environment** The objects or conditions by which somebody or something is surrounded

**estuary** A body of water formed where freshwater from rivers and streams flows into the ocean, mixing with the seawater

**fertile** Something rich in nutrients

**fuel cell** A battery-like device that releases energy. For example, in a hydrogen fuel cell, hydrogen and oxygen are combined to form energy and water

**geothermal** Energy from hot rocks below the surface of Earth

**global warming** A gradual rise in temperatures which is being caused by greenhouse gases trapping too much heat in Earth's atmosphere

**greenhouse gases** Gases such as carbon dioxide, nitrous oxide, or methane that are released into Earth's atmosphere when fossil fuels are burned

**infrastructure** The basic system of organization or structures, such as utilities, roads, or buildings, required for the operation of a society

**innovative** Something new that has not been done before

**Kyoto Treaty (or Kyoto Protocol)** An international agreement signed in Kyoto, Japan, in 1997. Its aim is to reduce greenhouse gas emissions around the world

**levee** An embankment constructed to prevent flooding

**ozone** A zone located about 9 to 30 miles (15 to 48 km) above Earth, that contains enough ozone (a form of oxygen) to block out most ultraviolet rays from the Sun

**photosynthesis** The process by which green plants take carbon dioxide and water and combine them using energy from sunlight to make sugar and oxygen

**pollution** The contamination of air, water, or soil by harmful substances, such as greenhouse gases, oil, chemicals, or garbage

**renewable** Something that will not run out, such as the Sun's energy or wind power, or something that can be replaced in a short amount of time, such as plants, trees, and animals

**sewage** The waste from toilets that is carried away in sewers

**silt** Deposits of sediment at the bottom of a river or lake

**"slash and burn"** A method of clearing land by cutting down, and burning, forested areas for agriculture

**suburbanization** The migration of people from a city center to the outskirts of a city, which is known as the "suburbs"

**sustainable** Using raw materials in such a way that their supply will continue into the future without causing environmental damage

**ultraviolet** A blue light that is invisible to humans

**urbanization** The formation and growth of cities, or urban areas, so that more people in an area live in the cities than in the rural areas

# IDEAS FOR DISCUSSION

- Palm oil is an important crop in many developing countries as it is used in many processed foods and as a renewable biofuel. However, rain forests are cleared to make way for new oil palm plantations. So is the growing demand for palm oil a good or a bad thing?

- The Three Gorges Dam on the Yangtze River in China is the world's largest hydroelectric dam. Hydroelectricity is a clean, renewable source of energy. The building of the dam has had a huge impact on the local environment, though. Discuss whether we should encourage the building of more dams in the world's rivers.

- As sea levels rise, coastal erosion will get worse. Should we spend money on defending the coast against erosion, or should we let nature take its course?

- Imagine the heavy congestion in your local city is polluting the atmosphere and damaging business as people cannot travel around quickly. The city planners want to build a new road around the outside of the city cutting through an important wildlife area. What do you consider to be more important, the quality of life for the people living in the city, or the wildlife habitat?

- Look around your local city. Is there congestion? Are there green spaces or renewable energy schemes? If you were a city planner how would you improve the environment? Could you reduce the city's energy needs? How would you save water or grow more food within the city?

# FURTHER INFORMATION

### www.sustainlane.com/us-city-rankings/
How sustainable is your city? Look at the rankings for the top 50 cities in the United States in 2008.

### http://vancouver.ca/sustainability/
Find out about the plans in Vancouver for a more sustainable city.

### www.inhabitat.com
Web site featuring eco news stories on sustainable living, green buildings, and much more.

### http://rooftopfarms.org/
Web site about a rooftop farm in Manhattan, New York.

# INDEX

# INDEX

## ABOUT THE AUTHOR

*Sally Morgan is a leading author of children's nonfiction with more than 200 titles to her name, covering science, natural history, and environmental topics. She studied Natural Sciences at Cambridge University which was followed by several years of research into the restoration of derelict land. Sally's interest in environmental issues and conservation led to a career in writing.*